OUR DIGITAL PLANET

Using Digital Technology

by Ben Hubbard

raintree

a Capstone company — publishers for children

Raintree is an imprint of Capstone Global Library Limited, a company incorporated in England and Wales having its registered office at 264 Banbury Road, Oxford, OX2 7DY – Registered company number: 6695582

www.raintree.co.uk
myorders@raintree.co.uk

Edited by Nikki Potts
Designed by Sarah Bennett
Picture research by Ruth Smith
Production by Laura Manthe
Originated by Capstone Global Library Limited
Printed and bound in India

ISBN 978 1 4747 3498 1 (hardcover)   ISBN 978 1 4747 3502 5 (paperback)
20 19 18 17 16   21 20 19 18 17
10 9 8 7 6 5 4 3 2 1   10 9 8 7 6 5 4 3 2 1

British Library Cataloguing in Publication Data
A full catalogue record for this book is available from the British Library.

Acknowledgements
We would like to thank the following for permission to reproduce photographs: Dreamstime: Tomnex, 10; Shutterstock: Bambax, 22 (e-book), Bloomua, 8, Gagliardilmages, 19, Georgejmclittle, 13, 22 (streaming), back cover left, Iryna Tiumentseva, 18, Monkey Business Images, 5, Nata-Lia, 4, Nednapa Sopasuntorn, 20, Nikolaeva, cover design element, interior design element, ProStockStudio, cover, Rawpixel.com, 6, 11, 17, 22 (cloud), 22 (download), scyther5, 22 (social media), sirikorn thamniyom, 12, Stefano Garau, 9, back cover right, Twin Design, 22 (application), Tyler Olson, 21 Uber Images, 16, Vinne, 14, waldru, 15; Thinkstock: AndreyPopov, 7

We would like to thank Matt Anniss for his invaluable help in the preparation of this book.

Every effort has been made to contact copyright holders of material reproduced in this book. Any omissions will be rectified in subsequent printings if notice is given to the publisher.

All the internet addresses (URLs) given in this book were valid at the time of going to press. However, due to the dynamic nature of the internet, some addresses may have changed, or sites may have changed or ceased to exist since publication. While the author and publisher regret any inconvenience this may cause readers, no responsibility for any such changes can be accepted by either the author or the publisher.

Contents

Some words are shown in bold, **like this**.
You can find them in the glossary on page 22.

How do we use computers?

Computers come in many shapes and sizes. Tablets, laptops and smart phones are all computers.

We use computers for many different reasons. We play games on computers. We can also use computers to help with schoolwork.

How do we connect with computers?

People connect in many ways using computers. We can write to each other using **social media**.

We can share files using email. We can also make voice and video calls with messaging programs.

What are programs and apps?

A computer runs a program to carry out a set of tasks. Special programs called **applications** let us listen to music, search the internet, write and save documents and more.

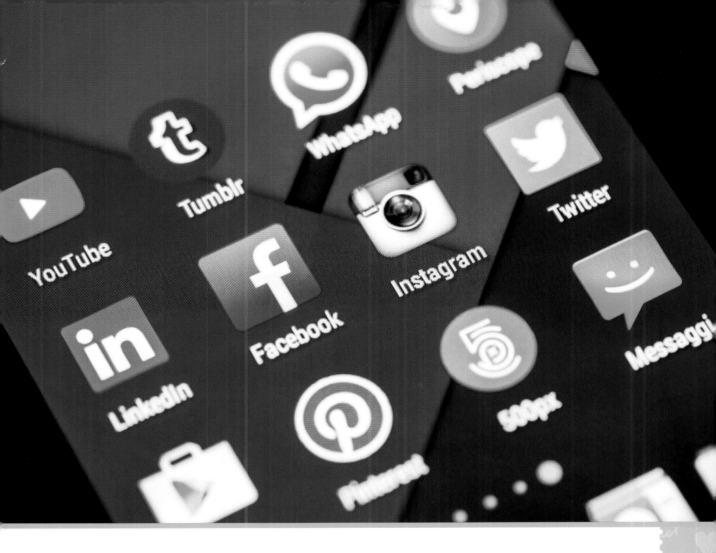

An "app" is an application for tablets and smart phones. Apps are usually simpler than programs designed for larger computers.

How do we use the internet?

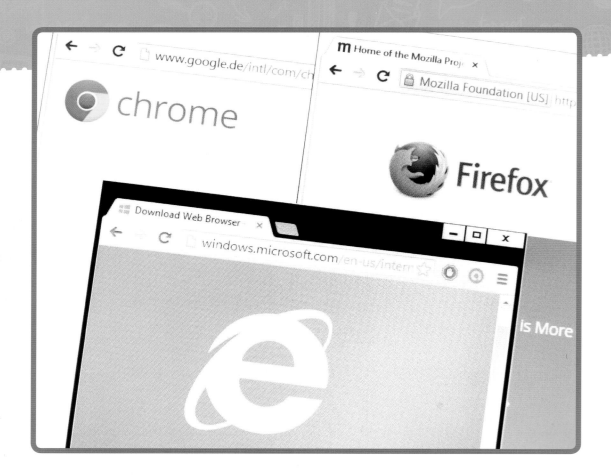

To visit a website, we type its web address into an **application** called a web browser. Some popular browsers are Firefox and Chrome.

We can also search for information by typing words into a search engine. Popular search engines include Google and Bing.

How do we get films and music?

Files such as music, films and **e-books** can be **downloaded** from the internet. We can store these files on our computers.

Music, films and television shows can also be "**streamed**" from the internet. You can watch or listen to streamed files whenever you like, but they cannot be stored.

Where do we store files?

Computers are like digital filing cabinets that store our files. We organize our files by putting them into folders. Files can also be stored in the "**cloud**".

We can then access our cloud files from anywhere, on any computer that is connected to the internet.

What are word and number files?

Many people use word processing **applications** to type documents on a computer. These text files can be created for school, home and work.

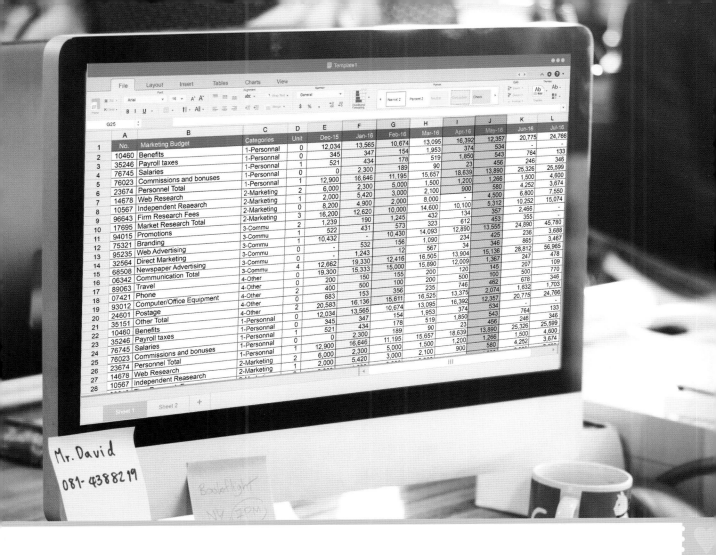

Spreadsheets are another type of file. They are used to store numbers and do maths.

How do we play games?

There are many different computer games. Some are action and sports games.

Others are puzzles and quizzes. Games can be played alone or with other people.

Can we design our own applications?

Some **applications** let us create our own music, films and artworks. There are even applications to design our own apps!

Many people start a career in computers by designing their own apps.

Glossary

 **application** computer program that performs a certain task

 **cloud** where information is kept on large computers; the information can be accessed from anywhere, anytime

 **download** transferring a copy of a file from the internet to your computer

 **e-book** electronic book that can be read on a computer

 **social media** form of online communication where users create online communities to share information, ideas, messages, etc.

 **streaming** sending sounds or moving pictures over the internet, straight to your computer

Find out more

Books

Clever Computers (Cambridge Reading Adventures), Jonathan Emmett (Cambridge University Press, 2016)

Digital Technology (Technology Timelines), Tom Jackson (Franklin Watts, 2016)

Understanding Computer Search and Research (Understanding Computing), Paul Mason (Raintree, 2016)

Websites

www.bbc.co.uk/education/subjects/zyhbwmn
This BBC website is designed to teach young learners about computers.

www.easyscienceforkids.com/all-about-computers/
This Easy Science For Kids website explains computers and their history.

www.factmonster.com/ipka/A0772279.html
This Factmonster website provides information and games about computers, technology and the internet for kids.

Index